too cute
Kittens

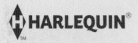

TOO CUTE KITTENS

ISBN-13: 978-0-373-89287-7

Library of Congress Cataloging-in-Publication Data

Too cute kittens / Animal Planet's most impossibly adorable kittens
    pages cm
  ISBN 978-0-373-89287-7 (hardback)
1. Kittens--Pictorial works. 2. Kittens--Miscellanea. 3. Cat breeds--Pictorial works.
I. Animal Planet (Television network)
  SF446T66 2013
  636.8'07--dc23
                                        2013024778

too **cute**
Kittens

Animal Planet's Most
Impossibly Adorable Kittens

ANIMAL PLANET

too cute Kittens

Kyra Lee, a **RagaMuffin** cat, needs all the rest and relaxation she can get. Her four adorable and very active kittens are keeping her moving.

The four RagaMuffin kittens have not even opened their eyes yet, but the littlest kitten, Otto, is already an adventurer. When he is done napping, nothing is going to hold him back!

Brandy is the only sister in the litter, and her brothers don't always let her play with them. But her human gives her plenty of special attention. It's impossible to resist lavishing love on a kitten with such a charming lounge act.

Affable and docile, RagaMuffins are not adept climbers. They would much rather keep a low profile. But not little Otto! He is the bravest kitten of his litter, defying all stereotypes and climbing to new heights.

Fluffy, cuddly RagaMuffins are descended from Ragdoll, Persian, Burmese and Angora cats. RagaMuffins by nature are relaxed and the kittens are growing up to be low-lying, loving, lap-hogging cats.

Although **Ocicats** look like miniature jungle cats (they especially resemble the spotted ocelots that they are named after) they are completely domestic. But don't tell that to Rex! This spunky kitten knows he's wildly adorable!

British Shorthairs are the most popular breed of cat in England and it's not hard to see why! Their gigantic eyes, adorably round faces and perfect smiles make them unbearably darling.

Things get dodgy when Brits have the run of the office.
Moose hasn't quite figured out how to answer client calls, but he knows how to keep the hotline warm.

One of these classy British Shorthair kittens will grow up to assist its mom working at a veterinary office. They will need to learn office skills, but for now they have their cute skills in the bag.

Pippa, sporting an elegant gray beret, has got it all! She has office skills, client skills and people skills. Everyone is certain she is the perfect cat for the job!

Tiny Dancer is an **Abyssinian,** an athletic sleek breed with origins in Africa.
The runt of the litter, she isn't quite big enough to dance yet,
but extra small treasures are even dearer.

The **Cornish Rex** were bred from a mutation found in Cornwall, England, in the 1950s. Sleepy Tofu may be a mutant, but he sure is a cuddly one!

These five Cornish Rex kittens are only four days old, but won't get much furrier. The short downy coat they are born with is said to be the softest of all cat breeds and a special kind of cute.

Timber, the German Shepherd,
may be surrounded by what looks
like a pack of pointy-eared prowlers,
but they're all just cozy kittens to her.

Cornish Rex are named after the Astrex rabbit, which has a similar short wavy coat. Although, these kittens are more like sleeping beauties than hurried hares.

There is no cozier spot for Tofu's nap than with his friend Timber.
When you don't have much fur, you find it where you can.

The Cornish Rex come in all colors, patterns and playful personalities. Whatever their hue, they are as delightful as they are darling.

Tofu is five weeks old and eventually his body will catch up with his oversize ears, but in the meantime, he is keeping an ear out for new friends and his forever home.

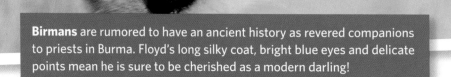

Birmans are rumored to have an ancient history as revered companions to priests in Burma. Floyd's long silky coat, bright blue eyes and delicate points mean he is sure to be cherished as a modern darling!

Cheetah is a **Savannah**, a breed created by crossing a domestic cat with the wild serval. He may look well behaved and innocent, but he's already on the prowl.

Toys are not just for fun, they are prey, and Cheetah's sister Cougar has her eye on the next "victim." No doubt she'll subdue it with one enthusiastic pounce.

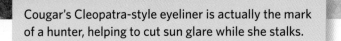

Cougar's Cleopatra-style eyeliner is actually the mark of a hunter, helping to cut sun glare while she stalks.

Savannahs are considered to be friendly and social cats. Tiger can't wait to spend time with her new family, who is sure to think she is wildly captivating.

Burmese cats once roamed the palaces and temples of Burma, but Pepper doesn't need to roam any farther than the couch to demonstrate her charm and ability to coax you into a cuddle.

Munchkins were bred in the 1980s from a mutation of stubby-legged cats. These cats may be small in stature, but Stretch proves they are larger than the average cat in cute!

Not all Munchkin kittens are born with short legs. These kittens model their long limbs, proving that statuesque can also be adorably fashionable.

Munchkins are outgoing and playful cats that are simply irresistible. Stretch is looking extra huggable today!

Porkchop and Nugget prove that all good things are more delightful in pairs. So this sweet set of shorties sticks together.

Munchkins come in a mixed bag of coat colors that are either silky and long or plush and short. With such a wide variety of possibilities, these cuties are sure to find the perfect families.

When everyone is looking at your legs, you may as well strut with them. Stretch demonstrates his best charming, on-the-catwalk sashay.

Even though they are closer to the ground, short-legged Munchkins are fast, active and can even jump quite high. Nugget may be vertically challenged, but she will leap right into your heart.

Maine Coons with their thick coats and snowshoe paws are always ready to keep you warm. They hit the U.S. shores from France over 200 years ago and have been romancing us ever since.

Orange cats, even Maine Coons
like Dante, are four times more likely
to be male. And Dante is four times
more likely to be lovable.

Zack's mom is a **Calico**, a Domestic Shorthair with a tricolor coat. Calicoes are almost always female, so Zack doesn't look much like her, but he makes up for it in looking extremely pettable.

The **Domestic Shorthair** is the most popular cat in America. A wide mix of colorful characters, these felines make up 95% of all pet cats. When it comes to cute, they've got the market covered!

Twins Boots and Little Bear are exploring their personal wilds and bringing a dose of delightful to the domestic jungle.

Little Bear is five weeks old and has tucked himself deep into the domestic outback while he waits for a new jungle where as king, he can rule with a cherished paw.

Himalayans are a loyal lap cat. Handsome, fluffy and cloud-white, Jacques is waiting for the perfect lap to while away his days.

Russian Blues have silver-blue coats and a mysterious history. They are said to have been companions to Russian czars. It's no mystery, however, that Sputnik is perfectly precious.

Sputnik is definitely an innerspace traveler and his first unexplored space is going to be the ground floor (when he figures out how to use the stairs).

Sputnik, along with his brother and two sisters, may have just recently opened their eyes and discovered their legs, but they are already experts at sweet sibling siestas.

Russian Blues are lean, elegant, smart cats that make wonderful family pets. You only have to take one look at this precious pile of royal fur to know they are blue-blooded.

When Sputnik finally makes it downstairs, he discovers a world filled with wonders.
Whatever new friends this fearless explorer discovers, they are sure to be captivated by his regal charm.

Of all the household wonders to be found, the kitchen is truly a kitten's paradise, always filled with unexpected treasures.

Eventually, Sputnik runs out of new territory to explore, but the exploits are not over. The best adventure is yet to come....

The **Sphinx** was bred from a type of cat with a natural mutation discovered in 1966. Completely bald, this breed's fans are enchanted by their irresistible personalities and a very different kind of lovable.

Sphinx cats, like Gremlin, have to be kept in a climate-controlled environment to stay warm when they are young. The kittens may take extra care, but beauty has a price, and bald is beautiful!

Sphinx cats come in two varieties, straight- and curl-eared. The cats with curled ears are called elfs and Gremlin is adorably elfin.

Siberians are the national cat of Russia, and although they come in a variety of colors, all have a lush, dense, three-layer coat. Although these short-coated kittens have a Siberian mother, they also look an awful lot like the handsome cat next door....

Socks and Mittens have a family who is anxious to adopt them. They may not look like Russian highborns, but they are undeniably enchanting.

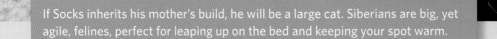

If Socks inherits his mother's build, he will be a large cat. Siberians are big, yet agile, felines, perfect for leaping up on the bed and keeping your spot warm.

These **Tabby** kittens were orphaned when they were only a few weeks old. But they were fortunate enough to find their way into a loving home where they met their new friend Nellie, a three-week-old orphaned skunk.

Singapuras are adaptable, spry cats that are big on climbing and jumping. Basil was the first of his litter to open his eyes, but Pepper and Saffron are right behind him and will soon be ready to leap into the new world.

It's not difficult to see where the Singapura kittens got their grace and good looks. Mom, Jasmine, is a feline charmer.

At five weeks old, the city Singapuras are all about stalking and catching prey. Toys are fun, especially when you can play with your siblings.

Saffron has learned that the best way to get attention is to stay out of trouble. She's looking for a quiet place and a cuddle.

Basil is always looking for more fun and adventure. It doesn't get much better than a tiny tunnel and an unexpected toy at the end.

These miniature athletes can't resist leaping to new heights.
Basil may be small in stature but the high jump is second nature!

Warm and trusting, **Ragdolls** are a breed that is always ready to melt into any loving lap. Bold Snowball is ready to find the perfect lap and stay forever.

The **Tonkinese** is a cross between Burmese and Siamese cats,
making the Tonkinese a breed with a charming sense of play and a chatty demeanor.

Queenie is a first-time mother with plenty of love to give. Tonkinese are born with white coats that darken over time, so it won't be long until her classy kittens have their mom's good looks.

These kittens have spent weeks getting
up to no good in the best way possible.
Now it's time to go to their forever homes.
They are sure to go to families that think
they are the cat's pajamas.

Tabby cats usually have striped coats and white socks. Although their coats can vary, they all have the letter "M" on their forehead, which is said to stand for "mao," Chinese for *cat*.

Muffin has two girls and two boys in her litter, an even mix of lovable. At four weeks old, the kittens know every comfortable position for napping and exactly how to be a perfect puzzle of precious.

Max is a classic Tabby with a love of climbing. He may be little, but he's already a leaping legend.

Paws likes his feet on the ground and is not too sure about climbing. All the same, he's willing to follow in Max's footsteps.

A little bit of adventure goes a long way for Paws. Staying on Max's tail has worn him out, but fortunately with three siblings, there is always someone willing to take a snooze.

Paws is a homebody and too irresistible not to keep. Even though he has plenty of suitors, he stays with Mom when his siblings find new homes. Who could say "no" to a face so sweet?

Exotic Shorthairs have the flat, round face of Persians with the short but luxurious coat of an American Shorthair. Mia is as darling as they come, especially after having her coat primped by Mom.

The **Toyger** is as domestic as they come, but when you cross a Bengal Tabby and a Domestic Shorthair Tabby, you get a cat with an exotic tigerlike coat. All the same, these kittens are most at home in a living room jungle.

Sparky and Tanya may be toy tigers, but they don't like to go it alone. Even when they are on the prowl, these two are inseparable.

Toygers were bred to raise awareness for their endangered and distant cousin, the tiger. Tigers may be struggling in the wild, but a kitten as irresistible as Sparky is sure to have a comfortable life and a ready lap.